Warren Hastings

An appeal to the people of England and Scotland, in behalf of

Warren Hastings

Warren Hastings

An appeal to the people of England and Scotland, in behalf of Warren Hastings

ISBN/EAN: 9783743347243

Manufactured in Europe, USA, Canada, Australia, Japa

Cover: Foto ©Lupo / pixelio.de

Manufactured and distributed by brebook publishing software
(www.brebook.com)

Warren Hastings

An appeal to the people of England and Scotland, in behalf of

Warren Hastings

AN

APPEAL

TO THE

PEOPLE

OF

ENGLAND AND SCOTLAND,

IN BEHALF OF

WARREN HASTINGS, Esq.

LONDON:

Printed for J. DEBRETT, opposite Burlington-
house, in Piccadilly.

————

MDCCLXXXVII.

A N

A P P E A L, &c.

WHEN the ambition of France openly
threatened Europe with univerſal mo-
narchy, the duke of Marlborough turned the
tide of ſucceſs, and, controlling fortune by the
ſuperiority of his genius, ſeemed to proceed,
by a ſure march, from fortreſs to fortreſs, to
the gates of Paris. But in the midſt of this
career of proſperity and glory, that military
ardour and high ſpirit of liberty, which had
lately ſhone forth among all ranks and orders of
men in England, was ſuddenly exchanged for a
rooted averſion to war, an anxious deſire of
peace, and a ſuperſtitious dread concerning the

ſafety

fafety of the church. The public admiration was transferred from the Duke of Marlborough to Dr. Sacheverell; from the great protector of the liberties of Europe, to a defpicable fire-brand of fedition. And while the Englifh nation almoft deified a pragmatical prieft, they feemed, in their undifcerning fury, to demand, as a victim at his altar, the very man who had raifed the Britifh name to the higheft point of elevation. All our hiftory is indeed full of tranfitions as quick, and of humours as unrea-fonable: but fince the reign of Queen Anne to the prefent times, there was none to be found fo much fitted to excite furprize, regret, and indignation, as the prefent perfecution of the Governor General of Bengal, nearly akin to the Duke of Marlborough, in character, in fituation, and in fate; except that the Commander in Chief of the confederated armies amaffed an enormous fortune; in which circumftance, too, Mr. Haftings might have eafily refembled him, if to preferve, fecure, and improve the Britifh dominions and influence in Afia had not been the predominant paffion of his foul, as he con-ceived it to be the firft duty of his ftation. But who can doubt, after the tranquillity enjoyed by fome late culprits at the bar of the Houfe of Commons,

Commons, and the folicitation of an interview with Major Scott on the part of a certain diftinguished orator *, that the prudential command of a great fortune, with the aid of lefs addrefs than

---

* This tranfaction was alluded to by Major Scott in his reply to Mr. Sheridan, which produced from Mr. Sheridan a very few words in anfwer: thefe went merely to imply, that Major Scott had acknowledged himfelf miftaken in his former account of the tranfaction. Major Scott may have a very good idea of Indian politics, but he has not fhewn himfelf a match for his opponents in England in point of manœuvre. To prevent the world, however, from entertaining an idea that the miftake made by Major Scott did at all affect the purpofe for which he has at any time alluded to this tranfaction, we fhall give the fact as it is, and leave our readers to draw their own conclufions from it.

On the 17th of November at night, Mr. Sheridan paid a vifit to a gentleman, who then lived in Berner's ftreet, and was known to have taken a very active part in favor of Mr. Haftings, in whofe family he had lived in India. This gentleman Mr. Sheridan had not vifited before this night for feveral months, and the intimacy between them, though not broken off perhaps, had long been fufpended. The exprefs avowed purpofe of this vifit, was to talk over the affairs of Mr. Haftings, and it was agreed between this gentleman and Mr. Sheridan, that the former fhould call on the next morning upon Major Scott, to communicate what had paffed, and Major Scott was to be defired to meet Mr. Sheridan at eleven o'clock that morning, at a third houfe. The communication made by the gentleman who

vifited

than Mr. Haſtings is allowed to poſſeſs even by his enemies, might have eaſily diverted the arrows of reproach, and ſecured an undiſturbed retreat from a life worn out in the ſervice of the

viſited Major Scott was, as he underſtood, that he came to him with the olive branch; that Mr. Haſtings might come home with perfect ſecurity, with his half million, or whatever might be the amount of his fortune; that the miniſters had ſtrength enough to carry the India bill, but that they knew it would be oppoſed at the India Houſe. The condition therefore required from Major Scott was, that the friends of Mr. Haſtings would not join in the oppoſition to the bill. In reply to this communication, Major Scott at once ſaid he would not meet Mr. Sheridan, but that he ſhould go to the gallery of the Houſe of Commons, where he ſhould hear Mr. Fox himſelf: and he further told the gentleman who called upon him, in anſwer to ſome doubts that were expreſſed whether Mr. Haſtings would come home when recalled, that all the world knew there had been a letter upon the table of the Court of Directors, ſince the month of September, in which he expreſsly deſired them immediately to appoint a ſucceſſor to the government of Bengal. The gentleman who waited upon Major Scott further told him, that, if the negociation came to nothing, no notice was to be taken of any offer of the kind having been made. Mr. Fox made his famous ſpeech on that day, the 18th of November, in which he grounded the neceſſity for his bill upon the miſmanagement of Mr. Haſtings, and ſaid his whole proceeding was the proceeding of a man who had

drawn

the public, and full of activity, trouble, and
danger?' That engine of defence he neither
poffeffed nor required. His own virtue was
the fhield which he oppofed to the fhafts of his
adverfaries,

drawn the fword, and thrown away the fcabbard. The fol-
lowing morning, the 19th, Major Scott, and the friend who
had called upon him, met again, when the latter clearly declared, that, after Mr. Fox's fpeech, Mr. Sheridan had no
right to expect fecrecy from either of them. The prefs was
not idle; every paper teemed with grofs and *anonymous* abufe
of Mr. Haftings, with threats of vengeance, and now and
then with fomething like a promife of favour, if the friends
of Mr. Haftings would be lefs active. In anfwer to one
of thefe paragraphs, Major Scott, not like a fkulking af-
faffin, who ftabs in the dark, but openly, and with his name
at full length to the affertion, publicly avowed, on the 27th
of November, ten days after Mr. Sheridan had vifited his
friend, that he, Major Scott, "*rejected the offer of an act of*
" *oblivion for his principal, provided he would remain filent*
" *during the prefent attack upon the Eaft India Company.*"
This avowal, written before the Committee of Proprietors at
the India Houfe, and inferted in the Morning Chronicle,
was never anfwered; nor was the gentleman whom Mr.
Sheridan had vifited, or Major Scott, taxed with a breach
of fecrecy.

In the month of March, 1786, two years and four
months afterwards, Major Scott again alluded to the circumftance in the Houfe of Commons. The allufion occa-
fioned a meeting between Mr. Sheridan and the gentleman
whom

adverfaries, in whom difappointed hopes, as the world conjectures, converted affected indignation into real refentment. And the fame magna-nimity which difdains the compromifes of con-fcious demerit will carry him triumphant through all his troubles.

The reafonings of his accufers, divefted of all adventitious ornaments, bear a nearer re-

whom he had vifited, and the confequence of that meeting was, a perfect agreement between Mr. Sheridan and that gentleman, that Major Scott had miftaken both the extent of the offer that was made, and the ground upon which it was made: but admitting the fact, as it muft be admitted where two gentlemen only were prefent during a converfa-tion, and agree exactly as to the particulars of it, what does the admiffion amount to? Not that Mr. Sheridan did not pay that gentleman a vifit the night before the day on which Mr. Fox brought in his bill---not that Mr. Sheridan did not agree to meet Major Scott the next morning---not that Mr. Sheridan did not fay Mr. Haftings might come home with fecurity, &c. It merely went to this, Major Scott was miftaken, firft, in believing that Mr. Sheridan's offer was made with the knowledge of Mr. Fox, and all the confidential men belonging to the Duke of Portland; and, fecondly, he was miftaken in fuppofing that the condition re-quired from him was that he and his friends fhould not op-pofe the India bill; whereas, in fact, all Mr. Sheridan wanted to know was this, whether the man who had written for a fucceffor would come home, if recalled under Mr. Fox's Bill?

femblance

femblance to the verbal difputes of ilogicians and cafuifts than the folid arguments of legiflators and ftatefmen ferioufly concerned for the welfare of the republic. In the whole compafs of morality there are two things principally to be confidered : Firft, what are the fentiments and what the tenour of conduct that denominates one action, or courfe of actions, virtuous, and the contrary vicious ? And, fecondly, by what principle or law is virtue recommended and authorized, and vice ftigmatized, and reprobated ? Concerning the laft of thefe queftions, metaphyficians have differed, and will for ever continue to differ ; but with regard to the firft and moft important, they are all of them very nearly, if not entirely agreed. If we examine all the writers on the law of nature, from Plato to Payley, we fhall find, that whatever the theories are with which they fet out, they all of them terminate in public utility and advantage. They affign, as the ultimate reafon for every rule which they eftablifh, the neceffities and the convenience of mankind, and readily admit that the firft and fundamental law in all political conftitutions is the prefervation of fociety *. On

* The great and good Mr. Locke, the affertor of the rights, and the expofitor of the nature of man, in what he
writes

On the profpect of war in general, it has uniformly been the practice of all countries, on
probable grounds of fufpicion, of which the executive branch of the legiflature always exercifed
the

writes on civil government, fays, that " Where the le-
" giflative and executive power are in diftinct hands (as
" they are in all moderated monarchies and well-framed
" governments), there the good of the fociety requires that
" feveral things fhould be left to the direction of him
" that has the executive power: for the legiflators not
" being able to forefee, and provide by laws, for all
" that may be ufeful to the community, the executor of
" the laws, having the power in his hands, has, by the com-
" mon law of nature, a right to make ufe of it for the good
" of fociety in many cafes where the municipal law has
" given no direction, till the legiflature can be conveni-
" ently affembled to provide for it. Many things there
" are which the law can by no means provide for, and thofe
" muft neceffarily be left to the difcretion of him that has
" the executive power in his hand, to be ordered by him
" as the public good and advantage fhall require: nay, it is
" fit, that the laws themfelves fhould in fome cafes give
" way to the executive power, or rather to this fundamen-
" tal law of nature and government, that, as much as may
" be, all the members of the fociety are to be preferved:
" for fince many accidents may happen wherein a ftrict
" and rigid obfervance of the law may do harm (as not to
" pull down an innocent man's houfe to ftop the fire when
" the next to it is burning); and a man may come fome-
" times,

the prerogative of judging, to fecure the perfons
of individuals thought to be difaffected to the
ftate, by which great public calamities are prevented. On the fame ground of public neceffity,
villages are deftroyed, left they fhould afford fhelter to the enemy. It is true, that in fuch cafes
reparation is made to the inoffenfive inhabitants:
and accordingly reparation has been made, notwithftanding the indications of an hoftile difpofition to the Englifh, on the part of the Princeffes

" times within the reach of the law, which makes no dif-
" tinction of perfons, by an action which may deferve re-
" ward and pardon. This power to act according to dif-
" cretion for the publie good, without the prefcription of
" the law, and fometimes even againft it, is that which is
" called prerogative, and, whilft employed for the benefit
" of the community, and fuitably to the trufts and ends of
" government, is never queftioned; for the people are
" very feldom or never fcrupulous or nice in the point.
" He that will look into the hiftory of England, will find
" that prerogative was always largeft in the hands of our
" wifeft and beft princes; becaufe the people, obferving
" the whole tendency of their actions to be the publie
" good, contefted not what was done without law to that
" end: or if any human frailty or miftake (for princes are
" but men made as others) appeared in fome fmall declina-
" tions from that end, yet it was vifible that the main of
" their conduct tended to nothing but the care of the pub-
" lic."

C of

of Oude, by Mr. Haftings, as far as the refumption of their jaghires is concerned. A provifion was made for replacing their income at the exact rate at which it had ftood in their own eftimate, while they held the jaghires, by making it the condition of the refumption, that they fhould receive a penfion equal to the amount of thofe poffeffions, in equal monthly payments; and thefe, for the fulleft fecurity, were made payable from the produce of the Company's affignments. Has the Britifh parliament, in which we find the men who held in their hands the reins of government, during that interefting conflict with fo many nations whofe afflicting confequences we all feel and deplore, and which has given birth to fo many charges and fo much recrimination, has the Britifh Miniftry and Parliament in all cafes made compenfation to thofe who have fuffered in the caufe of England, as ample, as equal, as permanent and fecure as that which the juftice of Mr. Haftings has granted to the Princeffes of Afia? The American Loyalifts, on the very fcene, braved the fury of prevailing rebellion with an intrepidity and conftancy that reproached that timorous and temporizing policy in Adminiftration, that indolence and infatuation

in

in the fervants of the crown both by fea and land,
and that cruel rage of faction, which impeded
the wheels of a weak government, in more forci-
ble ftrains than the moft piteous complaints that
could be poured forth before a generous people.
But what pen or tongue can defcribe the calamities which attended, and the horrors which
followed on the iffue of their noble conflict?
In what pathetic accents might not the inimitable
eloquence of Sheridan and Burke reprefent the
difconfolate widow, fitting in folitary places,
mourning an hufband flain, an infant loft * !
Or, if in the varying and fudden emo-
tions incident to the impaffioned foul, grief

" * She weepeth fore in the night, and her tears are on her
" cheeks: among all her lovers there is none to comfort
" her: all her friends have dealt treacheroufly with her,
" they are become her enemies. She is in bitternefs, when,
" in the days of her affliction and of her miferies, fhe re-
" membered the pleafant things fhe had in the days of old,
" when her people fell into the hands of the enemy and
" none did help her: when the comforter that fhould re-
" lieve her foul is far from her; when her children are de-
" folate becaufe the enemy prevailed; when the children
" and the fucklings fwoon in the ftreets of the city, and fay
" to their mothers, where is corn and wine? For they
" fwooned as the wounded in the ftreets of the city, and
" their foul was poured forth into their mothers bofom."

at

at the forrows of our fellow fubjects fhould be converted into indignation at the caufes from whence they fprung, what field for invective to the thunder of Fox! and what profound filence in the liftening fenate! while he devotes to deftruction the authors of fuch calamities, and in the heat of paffion, which throws all artifice at a diftance, almoft confeffes that the misfortunes of the Loyalifts are not wholly owing to the errors and the felfifh views of Adminiftration.

Amidft fuch candour and fincerity of fentiment, as fuch a fcene in the Houfe of Commons would infpire, could not all the logical diftinction of Mr. Pitt find fome precedent or pretext for ranking the mifconduct of Mr. Haftings, and the fufferings of women who have been reduced to the neceffity of accepting a yearly penfion from their fon, inftead of a landed eftate; might not, I fay, the fubtlety of Mr. Pitt find, if he pleafed, fome reafon for ranking the mifconduct of Mr. Haftings, and the grievances of the Begums, in an order inferior to the enormities that difgraced different parties in the conduct of the American war, and the cruel calamities that afflicted and ftill afflict the loyal fubjects of Great Britain acrofs the Atlantic? Does the pittance allowed by Government as an in-

demnification

demnification to the Loyalifts bear any proportion to the income continued to the Begums?
Ladies fecluded from the world in the receffes of
a feraglio, and in whofe hands political power
and importance ferved only, by nourifhing a fpirit
of ambition, to diffolve the ties of blood, and to
embitter the fallen ftate of their family by do-
meftic difcord? Far different from theirs is the
condition of the difperfed families of the
Loyalifts! Aged parents, accuftomed to receive
their kindred and friends with plenty and hofpi-
tality, now in the character of petitioners for
fome provifion againft the extremity of want for
themfelves and their children; and the tender
fex ftruggling by every effort to unite that delicacy and dignity of fentiment in which they have
been bred, with the means of felf-prefervation!
While fuch objects, related to us by blood, by
language, manners, and religion, by friendfhip
ill-requited on our part, and fond confidence
mifplaced on theirs; while fuch objects prefent
themfelves to our view, whence all this gallantry
to Bow Begum, and the women of the Haram
of Sujah ul Dowlah?

In the relation that fubfifts between fovereigns
and their fubjects, if allegiance is implied on the
one part, protection is prefumed on the other.

The

The Loyalifts, therefore, if the affairs of ftate, even on the greateft emergency, are to be fquared by the abftracted accuracy of eternal juftice and truth, have an undoubted right to an abfolute reftitution of all they have loft, and reparation, as far as that is poffible, for all they have fuffered. But is it argued that full reftitution as well as complete reparation to the unfortunate fubjects of Britain in America is impoffible? Then, it is admitted that political exigencies may not only fufpend, but fuperfede the execution of juftice. Under this conviction, then, let the candid mind judge of the conduct of Mr. Haftings refpecting the Begums of Oude and the Rajah of Benares.

It is a matter of notoriety, that by the example and at the inftigation of the Rajah Cheit Sing, the Zemindar of Benares, the inhabitants of that diftrict revolted from our government, and continued in a ftate of rebellion from the 22d of Auguft to the 22d of September, 1781. During that fhort but important period in which Mr. Haftings was confined to the Fortrefs and Plain of Chunar, and in a fituation which in the apprehenfion of many men portended certain deftruction to himfelf and his fmall party, the Begums of Fyzabad united their authority and influence to extend and aggravate the difficulties of the Englifh. Circular

letters

letters were written to the Zemindars of Oude, inciting them to rebellion ; rewards were proclaimed for the heads of Englifh officers and foldiers; a general revolt enfued, of which their agents were the principal leaders; the two chief eunuchs and confidential fervants of the younger Begum openly levied troops in the great fquare of the city, for the avowed fervice of Cheit Sing againft the Englifh, which were employed by the Rajah in his battles againft us. Thefe facts have been proved by the depofitions of Lieutenant Colonel Hannay, Major John Macdonald, Captain John Gordon, and many other witneffes, taken before Sir Elijah Impey, at Lucnow and Chunar, within three months of the time in which the events had paffed. Thefe, with other facts, are urged by Mr. Haftings in defence not only of a general refumption of the eftates, but alfo of the treafures in the poffeffion of the Begums, at the requeft of their fon and grandfon, the Nabob Affoph ul Dowlah, to whom they belonged by the right of hereditary fucceffion, and without the aid of which he could not fulfil his engagements to the Eaft India Company, which were abfolutely neceffary, by fupporting their, to maintain his own authority.

In oppofition to the truth of thefe facts, the
accufers

accusers of Mr. Haftings enter into a long and intricate train of reasonings, conjectures, imposing associations of ideas, witticisms, hyperbolical expressions, and even appeals to the majesty and justice of Heaven; shifting the ground on which the general issue of the question concerning the merit or the demerit of Mr. Haftings is to be rested, just as it suits their purpose.

1. At one time they demand legal evidence for the truth of what Mr. Haftings advances in his own vindication; and at another, when that evidence is adduced, they endeavour to turn the necessary steps by which it was obtained into ridicule, and to convert them into arguments of conscious guilt.

2. If the Governor reasons on the invariable principles of human nature, they decry vague conjecture, and are not satisfied with any arguments not founded on solid facts; if facts are produced, they affirm, that these could not have happened, as they appear to them to be contrary to the general principles of human nature.

3. They pervert even the sagacity of the Governor General to their purposes. They suspect and condemn him for acting from the convictions of his understanding, even when these were justified by subsequent events, and where the conduct to
which

which they led was indifpenfably neceffary to the falvation of the Englifh power in Afia.

4. If he ufes rigorous meafures, he is cenfured; but if, towards the fame perfons in the fame circumftances, he ufes lenity and indulgence, he is alfo accufed.

5. If he takes fhelter in the general principles of jurifprudence, they object to general queftions and confiderations on a complicated fubject; if he enters into a detail of facts, and fhews that fuch was the ftate of affairs, that no other meafures than thofe adopted could have reftored and fecured the public fafety, they drag him from the field of battle into the monaftic cell, array him in the habit of an Auguftin Friar, and try him by laws which, though fublimated from a congeries of facts in the imaginations of metaphyficians, cannot in all cafes be reduced to practice, confiftently with the great ends of political fociety.

6. To all thefe inftances of prejudice and egregious injuftice they add the enormity of reducing to the meafure of the Britifh laws and conftitution, the adminiftration of a magiftrate who had been fent in the name of his country to govern a people in fentiments, manners, and modes of life fo different from our own, that our laws and cuftoms are their abhorrence; in cir-

D   cumftances

cumftances of unparallelled difficulty and danger, and at a time when the projects for the government of India, formed at home, were perpetually changing, and every packet from England to Bengal carried out orders, not only contradictory to preceding orders, but inconfiftent with themfelves, and the whole taken not feverally, but in conjunction, impracticable.

Thefe are the charges which I bring before the people at large againft the accufers of Mr. Haftings; and on all of thefe I proceed farther to fpeak in their order.

Mr. Sheridan not only alledged that there was no legal evidence of the Princeffes of Oude being in a ftate of rebellion, but that there were no fair prefumptions of their delinquency, or that they entertained hoftile defigns againft the Englifh. To reports and hearfays, even in circumftances full of alarm, he paid no manner of regard. Now, if the chief magiftrate or governor of a province is not juftifiable in exerting the power committed to him for crufhing the infancy of a rebellion before he has legal proofs of its exiftence, why does Mr. Sheridan attempt to throw odium and ridicule on the Governor General for doing that which he himfelf requires, and what

the

the laws of England would have prefcribed in any fimilar cafe? That is, ufing the beft evidence that could be obtained, and giving it the beft poffible fanction. Can that be ridiculous which is wife and neceffary? If it can, then ridicule is not a proof that the conduct of Mr. Haftings, in taking the evidence in queftion before the firft Britifh judge in India, was unneceffary: if it cannot, and that Mr. Sheridan fhall contend that the conduct of Mr. Haftings and Sir Elijah Impey, in collecting evidence that a rebellion, though in its firft ftage, exifted in the province of Oude, as well as in that of Benares, furnifhed real and genuine matter of ridicule, then was not their conduct neceffary and proper; and a cafe may exift when the man in whofe hands his country entrufts her diftant and deareft interefts, may act in difcharge of his truft without obferving legal forms. And, if this be fo, it muft be admitted, that, in proportion as Mr. Sheridan was fuccefsful in his endeavours, which in reality formed no inconfiderable portion of his fpeech, to throw ridicule on the Governor General and Chief Juftice of Britifh India, in that proportion exactly does he vindicate the conduct of Mr. Haftings; if, in over-awing and checking the beginning of commotion, he ftepped beyond the

caution

caution of an Attorney, and, affuming the free-
dom of an honeft man, acted up to the character
with which he was invefted. In truth, it appears
to the common fenfe of mankind, as it did to
Mr. Haftings himfelf, that an exceffive anxiety
about *legal evidence*, in the circumftances in
which *he* was deftined to act, or his *country* to
fuffer, would indeed have juftly feemed an object
of ridicule. He did what a due regard to pru-
dence on the one hand, and decorum on the other,
naturally dictated to a firm and difcerning mind.
He authenticated his proofs before a Britifh magiftrate, and chiefly by Britifh fubjects. And
here it is to be obferved, that if Mr. Haftings
had been confcious of any degree of guilt, or
improper bias on his mind, he would naturally
have been fedulous to heap proof upon proof
of his innocence: dignity of mind would have
fhrunk before an apprehenfion of danger, and the
anxiety of the criminal would have been a plen-
tiful fource of the darkeft fufpicions that could
poffibly fpring up in an imagination fertile even
to excefs, and which can fupply in abundance
theories and conjectures to cover and protect
whatever doctrine or fact he chufes to eftablifh.
The gentleman to whom I allude I firmly believe to be naturally humane, benevolent, and
juft;

juft; but the fineft genius and the moft generous difpofition is not unufually found in conjunction with an irritability of temper which
magnifies its object. And when once the will
begins thus to influence the judgment, fertility
of invention, inftead of being a lamp of light,
becomes an *ignis fatuus* that leads into error.
It will never be forgotten, while the prefent im-
peachment fhall remain on our records, that the
apologift of *Powel* and *Bembridge* was the accufer
of WARREN HASTINGS.

But to return to Mr. Sheridan. Was it natural, decorous, and proper, if he either believed
that Mr. Haftings deferved bonds, imprifon-
ment, or death, or hoped to make it appear that
he did, to fet the Houfe at every turn of his
reafoning into a roar of laughter, and to convert
a criminal trial into a fcene of amufement?
However natural it may be for Mr. Sheridan to
turn tragedy into comedy, it was as unfair as it
was unnatural, to pour forth on the object of his
arraignment at once the torrent of ridicule and
of invective: for I fear that not a few of his
audience beftowed, as a reward on his wit and
humour, what they could not concede to the
force of his arguments. The indecent plaudits
heard at the conclufion of his humorous ha-
rangue,

rangue, difgraced the affembled fenate ; though, indeed, they were fit enough expreffions of that fpecies of fatisfaction which we derive from A SCHOOL FOR SCANDAL.

Very different from that *fupplofio pedis* which was practifed not by the orator, but the judges, was the deportment of the gallery, in which different individuals, when Mr. Pitt declared himfelf againft Mr. Haftings, expreffed their concern and furprize in involuntary exclamations, which of courfe incurred a rebuke from the Speaker. The fpectators of what paffed in the Houfe below, were not fo much touched with the humour of Mr. Sheridan, as with indignation that fuch talents fhould be mifpent in fuch a caufe.

There was nothing in the teftimonies of different gentlemen in the fervice of the Company in favour of Mr. Haftings impoffible, nothing inconfiftent, nothing contradicted by oppofite evidence: but it was alledged that what they affirmed was improbable, and that they were under the influence of Mr. Haftings, by whom they had either been obliged, or from whom they expected future favours. There was nothing advanced againft the evidence in proof of the rebellious defigns at Fyzabad that would be fuftained as a bar to its validity in an ordinary

court

court of juftice. But certain country gentlemen, and others affembled in the Houfe of Commons, under the aufpices of a rector of an univerfity *, a very witty author for their principal, and a ftudent from Cambridge for their *regius profeffor*, undertook to invalidate it on the moral prin- ciples of the human mind. They objected to general reafoning, and required pofitive proofs : pofitive proofs being brought, they return to general reafoning on the nature of man, and the motives that influence his conduct in different fituations. Having returned a fecond time to this ground; on this ground, in the name of the God of Truth, let the difpute be decided.

It is not credible, fay they, that an infurrec- tion fhould be raifed, or a war meditated againft the Englifh, whofe power had been fo recently and vifibly difplayed in dethroning or reftoring princes, and exterminating nations, by two weak women fecluded from the world in the inmoft receffes of an Eaftern feraglio. Is it then by bodily ftrength and perfonal prowefs, as in the favage ftate of fociety, that either kings or queens wage war in Afia or in Europe ? Was it of any confequence in the confederate war, whe-

* Mr. Burke is or lately was rector of the univerfity of Glafgow.

ther

ther the Sovereign of Great Britain, or, in the laſt Turkiſh war, whether the Sovereign of Ruſſia, was of the maſculine or feminine gender? But the very circumſtance of their deep retirement, and the delicacy of oriental manners, afforded a ſecurity to their perſons, which did more than counterbalance the want of manly vigour. What opinion can our orators entertain of the underſtandings of thoſe whom they thus angle and inveigle with the illuſions of puerile fancy? It was not the ſex, nor the age of the Begums that Mr. Háſtings was to conſider, but the numbers of men that were at their devotion; the prevalence and ſtrength of the principle that might unite theſe in action; the reſources that might enable them to elude our forces, to prolong the war, to take advantage of the favour, and to weary out by perſeverance the adverſity of fortune; and, above all, their diſpoſition to revolt, and the circumſtances that might encourage them to excite rebellion.

Whoever imagines that by all the mildneſs we have mixed, or that it is poſſible for us to mix with our tyranny over the natives and princes of Aſia, we ſhall be able to gain their confidence and affection, is egregiouſly miſtaken. Whatever aromaticks we may infuſe in their bitter cup, the

the bitter tafte will ftill fo far prevail as to induce a ftrong defire of cafting it from them whenever they can: and the greater the hope of being able to do fo, the more ardent alfo will be the defire. It is a property in human nature, that any emotion which attends a paffion is eafily converted into it, though in their natures they be originally different, and even contrary to each other. Hence hope is able not only to inflame the defire of obtaining any particular object, but alfo to excite anger againft the perfon who with-holds it, or to heighten it where it was before-hand the predominant paffion; agreeably to that faying of the poet Virgil, *fpes addita fufcitat iras*. To govern reduced provinces, efpecially fuch as are remote from the feat of government, by flackening the curb of power, and granting a few indulgencies to a fubjected people, imperious nations have always found to be difficult, and for the moft part impoffible. After what has fo recently paffed in America and in Ireland, we cannot be at a lofs to judge of the effects of partial conceffion. Every degree of liberty indulged to men tends to produce at once a defire, and a fenfe of their natural right to enjoy it in its full extent.

Mr. Francis faid, that it was through the old

E   Begum

Begum that the right of dominion and property in Oude defcended, fhe being the daughter and only heir of the antient Soubah. This Princefs, he added, was in fact, at leaft in right, the real Sovereign of Oude. She is allowed to be a woman of an high fpirit; and her pride is naturally heightened by the recollection of her anceftry, and of former times; fhe, therefore, confidered the Englifh as the oppreffors of her family, and the ufurpers of its inheritance. The refentment which fhe naturally entertained againft our nation, there was reafon to dread, would be inflamed by the hope of gratification. She was not uninformed of the fituation of affairs in the weftern world. The crowns of that monarch, whofe power fhe had long equally dreaded and detefted, feemed now to totter on his head; and that of America had already fallen. The French, the Spaniards, the Dutch, the three greateft maritime powers in the world next to ourfelves, and whofe ftrength was but too well known in the eaft, preffed with their united weight on the Englifh, and the ftandard of revolt began to be raifed in Benares. In fuch circumftances what confidence could Mr. Haftings repofe in the attachment of the high-fpirited Begum, or what in her numerous fubjects? Mankind are governed

by

by opinion; and the opinion by which they are governed is two-fold: an opinion of intereft, and an opinion of right. Ideas of right have an influence on the minds of men which have been found, in fome inftances, to prevail over thofe of intereft. Hence in all nations, and in none more than in Great Britain, Chiefs have been found, who, in the full poffeffion of their privileges and fortune, have flown to the ftandard of exiled princes, followed by bands of voluntary vaffals. But in Afia, where the reverence to royal blood is ftronger than in Europe, and where the oppreffions of Europeans, compared with thofe the people fuffer under their native princes, are greater ; in Afia, where all ranks of men are divided againft us by an opinion both of right and intereft, and ready to ftart into a pofture of hoftility on every occafion where there is any profpect of fuccefs, and in circumftances fo full of alarm, why fhould Mr. Haftings deem it incredible that the Princeffes of Oude fhould join the general confpiracy of the world againft Great Britain, or feek for theories by which he might reconcile hoftile appearances with benevolent intentions ? Is not our government over the natives of India, whatever palliatives we may apply or project, in reality defpotic ? Is not the

firft

firſt principle of deſpotiſm, jealouſy of its ſub-
jects? Was there no ground of jealouſy, jealouſy heightened beyond the pitch of its uſual
vigilance, in the circumſtances in which the Governor General of Bengal was placed towards
the cloſe of the year 1781? If there was, is his
country, which his ſervices have ſo eminently
contributed to ſave, to make no allowance for
the force, for the violence with which reports of
military preparations muſt have fallen on a mind
anxious for the preſervation of all that was committed to the exertion of its powers? On the
one hand, it was at leaſt probable that a revolt
was begun in the province of Oude as well as in
Benares, and more than probable that it was
intended: on the other, it was poſſible that the
reports concerning the orders and deſigns of the
Begums might be falſe. In this dilemma, ye
accuſers of Mr. Haſtings, what would ye have
done? If his fears ſhould prove to be ground-
leſs, and that, in ſeizing the reſources of the Begum, he ſhould commit an injury, that injury
might afterwards be repaired; but if, on the
preſumption that their intentions, notwithſtanding all appearances to the contrary, were pacific,
he ſhould forbear to act as he did, the empire
of Great Britain in the Eaſt might be loſt.

In

In our wars with the Houſe of Bourbon, have we not been accuſtomed, on the appearance of hoſtilities on the part of that kingdom, to anticipate an attack by making one? Is this conduct to be condemned? Are the miniſters who followed it with ſucceſs to be impeached, and thoſe who, notwithſtanding the communications from Lord Stormont when ambaſſador at Paris, neglected it to the diſgrace of Britain, to be promoted and honoured? Was not the conduct of Mr. Haſtings exactly in the ſpirit of the great Earl of Chatham? And whether are we to reprobate the memory of the father, or to approve the *legal policy* of the ſon; who, as if he were born to refute the doctrine that the qualities of the mind are hereditary as well as thoſe of the body, condemns in Mr. Haſtings what raiſed his progenitor to immortal honour?

It will not be ſaid that the Earl of Chatham acted improperly, when, being apprehenſive of the deſigns of Spain, by a ſudden blow, he prevented their execution. Yet there was no overt act on the part of the Spaniards, no declaration of intended hoſtilities. What then is the circumſtance, or what the circumſtances of diſcrimination between the two caſes of Lord Chatham and Mr. Haſtings, which juſtify the conduct

duct of the former, and condemn that of the latter? · It may be faid, that the Begums of Oude
were living under the protection of our friend
and ally, or, to fpeak the truth, that they were
in fact our fubjects : and it alfo may be faid, that
the danger to which Great Britain was expofed
from Spain, was greater than that which was
threatened by the Begums. Befides thefe, there
is no circumftance of diftinction between the
two cafes of Chatham and Haftings, which can
affect in the fmalleft degree the queftion' at
iffue.

Though the Begums of Oude lived under the
protection of our ally, and were in fact our fubjects, they were divided from the Englifh by all
thofe circumftances of diverfity which commonly
prove the fources of animofity and conteft among
nations. Though overborne by fuperior power,
the unconquerable will remained of fhaking off
the Englifh yoke; and who, reafoning on the principles of the law of nature, will affirm that they
had not a right to fpurn it, if they could? The
very circumftance of their fubjection was a reafon
why we fhould be jealous of their endeavours to
overturn it. There were more points of oppofition between them and the Britifh nation, than between the Britifh nation and the Spaniards: and
their

their minds were at least equally hostile. What is the magic then, in the name of God, of their being our friends, allies, or subjects, that should supersede the propriety of considering what are their real inclinations, and what their power in all situations when vigilance becomes the first duty of a statesman, when jealousy becomes a virtue? The only question is, concerning the different degrees of the dangers which threatened Great Britain from the Spaniards in 1762, and from the Princes of India in 1781. And here an opportunity is presented of displaying the striking contrast between the glorious successes of the English arms in the former period, and the misfortunes which menaced our independence in the latter. But it is superfluous to dwell on so fertile a theme. For who that, dismissing the illusions of the imagination, yields to the conduct of his understanding, does not perceive the absurdity and injustice of applauding the vigour, promptitude, and prevention of the Earl of Chatham in times of national splendour unsullied by a cloud, and condemning the same qualities and a similar course of conduct in Mr Hastings, when condensing storms seemed ready to wreck the state on rocks and shoals, or overwhelm it in the troubled ocean? As to the comparative evidence on which an apprehension of hostilities

on

on the part of the Spaniards, and on that of the Begums of Oude, was founded, there was no overt act of hoftility, which Mr. Pitt declared to be neceffary, in order to afcertain hoftile intentions, that could be charged and proved againft either. But both had made military preparations, reports in both cafes had prevailed of hoftile intentions, and in both the circumftances of the times were fuch as to render thofe reports highly credible. The reports in India which Mr. Sheridan treated as vague, fortunately for this country, made that impreffion on the mind of Mr. Haftings, which they were naturally fitted to make on a found underftanding and a refolute mind ; and that impreffion was afterwards juftified by evidence on oath before the chief Britifh magiftrate in India.

But the enemies of Mr. Haftings obferve, that this evidence was pofterior to the actions which prefuppofed them; and they contend that whatever pretenfions Mr. Haftings may have to penetration, and however fortunate the meafures he purfued, he did not act towards the Begums on legal evidence, even fuppofing the teftimonies produced to have been unqueftionable, which they deny. Suppofe that Mr Haftings had been placed in fuch a fituation as to have over-heard a converfation involving rebellious defigns, and fixing the

meafures

meafures for carrying them into execution, between
the Begums and their confidential fervants, but
that he was the only perfon in the world that ever
had any reafon to fufpect fuch defigns, or to be made
acquainted with the meafures propofed for effecting
them; would he have acted in an unjuftifiable manner, if he had fruftrated their intentions by cutting
off the means of fulfilling them? Mr. Haftings, from
his knowledge of the country, the people, and the
circumftances of the day and hour, muft be allowed to have been a better judge of the credit due
to the reports that prevailed of the defigns of the
Begums, than any perfon in Great Britain at the
prefent moment, at fo great a diftance of fpace
and time. It appeared by fubfequent difcoveries
that he judged rightly. How ridiculous then is
it to condemn him for acting according to the
dictates of his underftanding, when thefe were
afterwards proved to have been wholly conform-
able to the truth?

But in order to weaken the evidence that was
produced in proof that his convictions concerning
the defigns of the Begums were in fact conform-
able to the truth, the accufers of Mr. Haftings
enter at great length into the fituation of the witneffes, and the nature of their evidence. The
witneffes, they fay, were men on whom he had

F   beftowed,

beſtowed, or on whom he might beſtow favours; or who, from whatever cauſe, were attached to his perſon. There, it muſt be owned, they have a field of objection to all the teſtimony that can be brought in vindication of his conduct: for the ſublimity of his genius had gained an aſcendency over the underſtandings, and the generoſity of his diſpoſition, and the unaſſuming modeſty of his manners, had won the hearts of all whom arrogance and rivality had not rendered blind to his exalted talents and virtues, and indifferent, nay, inimical to the proſperity of their country, if it depended on his exertions, or was connected with his name. It may naturally be ſuppoſed, therefore, that as the Britiſh in India, in general, would be forward to bear teſtimony in favour of the Governor-General, ſo the few who might be otherwiſe diſpoſed, would be willing to avoid a contrary conduct: yet the popularity of any Commander or Chief cannot certainly be urged as a legal objection to evidence in his favour, if that evidence bears no internal marks of falſehood. The facts alledged amount to a clear proof of both rebellious deſigns and actions, and the teſtimonies by which they are ſupported are ſufficient both with regard to numbers and reſpectability. The ſlight difference between the

teſtiteftimony of Sheikh-Mahomed Aumeen Mheir, the fecond officer in the fervice of Cheit Sing, and that of Colonel Hannay, and the other Eng-lifh officers; the firft, fuppofing the troops fent to the Rajah to have been fent from Luc-now, the laft knowing them to have been fent from Fyzabad, but all agreeing that one thou-fand fwordfmen were fent by orders of the Be-gums; the flight difference, I fay, between thefe teftimonies, difagreeing in an immaterial circum-ftance, but perfectly coinciding in the point for which they were produced, inftead of invalida-ting, corroborates their joint evidence, as it is a clear proof that it was not preconcerted. But the grand objection to the vindication of Mr. Haftings, as written by himfelf, in what Mr. Sheridan calls his firft and fecond Defences, is, that the chain of evidence is not brought up from the commandant in the fervice of Cheit Sing, and from Colonel Hannay and the other Englifh officers, through every intermediate link, to the Begums iffuing orders to their eu-nuchs in the receffes of the feraglio. Who told the Moorifh Commandant, and the Englifh of-ficers, that circular letters were written to the Zemindars of Oude, inciting them to rebellion; that rewards were proclaimed for the heads of

Englifh

Englifh officers, foldiers, and fepoys; and that
all this was done in confequence of orders from
the Begums? What Zemindar, Polygar, or
Ryot? Specify his name and place of refi-
dence. Tell us precifely what he faid, and
where, and when. If not, we fhall hold your
evidence in favour of Mr. Haftings as carelefs,
vague, irregular, irrelevant, and unfatisfactory.
This is their great fortrefs. In this they triumph.

. It has been obferved above, that confcious
rectitude is not curious about the means of felf-
juftification, and that exceffive anxiety about ex-
culpation is not unnaturally conftrued into a
fymptom of guilt. Or, if the accufers of the
Governor, when they touched on this point,
happened to be in a merry vein, what a field,
as Mr. Haftings very juftly obferves, for triumph
and derifion would he have afforded to his accufer, had he exhibited the names of unknown
witneffes attefted by Cauzees of uncertain exiftence! Might it not, too, have been very plau-
fibly alledged, that the Governor General, in the
plentitude of his power, was able to extort from
individuals what declarations, and from the
lawyers of the country whatever attefations
he pleafed? Thefe confiderations are fufficient

to

to account for the neglect on the part of Mr,
Haftings and his friends to collect and record
the names of the witneffes on whofe teftimony
prompt meafures were taken for quafhing in good
time the defigns of the Begums of Oude. But,
left all thefe reafonings fhould prove unfatisfactory, and that the omitting to mention, or the
concealment, if they pleafe, of the names of the
Zemindars who acquainted the fervants of the
Company with the defigns of the Princeffes,
fhould fofter injurious fufpicions, Mr. Haftings
and his friends, and all who are concerned to
inveftigate the truth in this matter, may fafely
reft the iffue of the whole caufe on this queftion;
Can a fufficient reafon be given why the Englifh
officers in the evidence they gave before Sir
Elijah Impey, fhould ftudioufly conceal the
names of the Zemindars from whom they re-
ceived intelligence of what was tranfacted and
intended in the province of Oude?

There is no perfon, however independent in
fortune, that can bear to be fhut out from the
fympathy and fociety of his fellow-men. To be
frowned on by every countenance, to be regarded
with averfion and abhorrence by every eye, is a
ftate of mifery and defpair from which there is not
an human being who would not willingly take
fhelter

fhelter in the filent grave: but he who fhould have held an eftate or farm, or any poffeffion in the province of Oude, and at the fame time have appeared in character of an informer againft the Begums, would have been exiled from the fociety and the affectionate regards of his fellow-men, and become an object of univerfal hatred and execration. Mr. Sheridan puts the queftion, Is it natural to fuppofe that the Zemindar, or native Hindoo of whatever denomination, fhould wifh to have it concealed, that he had done a fervice to the Prince, his new mafter, and to the victorious and flourifhing Englifh? Would he not rather boaft of his merits, and look for protection and reward? No. Conftituted like other men, endowed with the common feelings of humanity, there is no reward which he would put in competition with a total exclufion from human fociety.—A reward of thirty thoufand pounds was offered after the battle of Culloden, 1746, to the man that fhould deliver up or difcover the Pretender, who wandered for many months in the Highlands and iflands of Scotland; yet was there not found a man, among thoufands ftruggling with poverty and want, who would relieve his fufferings by the price of blood. The Highlanders are an inoffenfive, humane, and generous

race

race of men; yet it is not to be fuppofed that there was not one among fo great a number who would not have yielded to fuch a temptation, if he had not dreaded, as worfe than poverty, or any evil from which wealth could fecure him, the univerfal abhorrence of mankind. In London the reward would have operated on the minds of thoufands, becaufe in the obfcurity of that immenfe capital thoufands of wretches are to be found who can fkulk from the face of their former acquaintance, and in new alleys and lanes efcape the condemnation of their infamy. This was not the cafe in the Highlands of Scotland; nor yet in the Zemindaries of Oude. The Zemindar or Ryot who fhould have difcovered any fact that might affect the fortune or the dignity of the Begums, if it had been known that he difcovered it to his neighbours, would have found life infupportable; while, at the fame time, various motives may be conceived that might have induced him to court the favour, and even to wifh for the ftability of the Englifh Government. Is it any wonder, then, that the natives or fubjects of Oude, who communicated intelligence of the rebellion to the Englifh officers, fhould defire that their intelligence might be kept fecret? Or is it a wonder that Englifh officers fhould keep their plighted faith to the Zemindars

dars who committed their future happiness into their hands? It would seem, that no inconsiderable part of the accusation brought against Mr. Hastings, and those who acted with and under him, is founded on their very virtue.

As the good faith and humanity exercised towards the Zemindars and others, who gave intelligence, has been converted into a subject of suspicion, so also has the lenity and forbearance shewn to the eunuchs and confidential servants of the Begums, after the discovery of their treasures. The treasures discovered, says Mr. Sheridan, the eunuchs are set at liberty, and all persecution of their mistresses immediately ceases: Does this look like an inquiry into a preconcerted rebellion, or an act of deliberate rapacity? If Mr. Hastings had continued to press down the load of suffering, if the eunuchs had been thrown into dungeons, and outrages committed against the Begums, a court of inquisition instituted, and evidence invited, or even extorted; then would Mr. Hastings have escaped the imputation of interrupting severities the moment the end was obtained for which they had been applied; but he would have also forfeited the praise which is due to the magnanimous moderation of his conduct. " Enough had been
" done

" done for the reftoration of the Nabob's autho-
" rity, and for the fecurity of the peace of his
" country; enough had been done for an exhibi-
" tion of example." It is unfair to judge of Mr.
Haftings' actions taken fingly and by themfelves.
We ought to view them as they are performed 'in
fucceffion, and combined to a falutary purpofe.
Mr. Haftings confulted at once his own feelings
and the ends of his adminiftration, when, with the
meafures that he judged to be neceffary for fupporting the authority of the Nabob, he united refpect for the fex and a regard to the neceffities of
the mother and grandmother of our princely
ally. And, on the whole, let the world judge,
whether ever any Governor, viceroy, or prince,
who had fo difficult a part to act as Mr. Haftings,
mingled greater refpect to the feelings and rights
of human nature, with that fyftem of conduct
which was neceffary to maintain the authority of
Government. This, this is the grand and deci-
five point on which Mr. Haftings ought to be
tried by his country, and on which he will be
tried, and juftified too, if not by his country that
reaps the fruits of his faithful fervices, yet by the
common fenfe and juftice of all civilized nations,
but by none more readily than that enlightened ·
people, whofe inordinate ambition his meafures
fo effectually reftrained.

This did not escape the shrewdness of Mr. Sheridan. It was therefore the consideration of this point, with which he set out in his artful, entertaining, and prolonged oration. Mr. Dempster had put some questions to the witnesses at the bar tending to ascertain that extremity of danger which was threatened by the long arrears due to the army. Mr. Sheridan animadverted on those questions with great rhetorical emotion, and contended that no political necessity whatever can vindicate an act of injustice. On the same and on other subjects Mr. Fox has at different times exclaimed in the House of Commons, *fiat justitia, ruat cœlum*; a maxim which, as a writer of distinguished reputation justly observed, would be an absurd sacrifice of the end to the means. As matters of fact always exist before law, and laws are never so numerous as cases, new conjunctures must sometimes arise, in which it is absolutely necessary to act according to the supreme law of the general advantage. And the purest moralists as well as theologians, have concurred in opinion, that a case may exist in which it is even " expedient that one " man should die for the people." Even the Stoic philosophy, from an enthusiast in which Mr. Fox borrows, and Mr. Sheridan takes the occasional use of that glowing expression

just

juft quoted, admits that the intereft and the very life of an individual member may be juftly facrificed on certain emergencies for the good of that body of which he forms a part. Laws arife out of the mixed ftate of human affairs: human affairs, in their prefent ftage, are not fquared to the abftracted nicety of pre-exiftent laws. Mr. Sheridan and Mr. Fox would not be fo great *Stoics* as to carry their doctrine into practice, if Providence fhould place them in a fituation in which it would be neceffary for them either to adhere to their maxim, or to ruin, not heaven and earth, but even that narrow fpot called Great Britain.

Vincit amor patriæ, laudumque immenfa cupido.

Suppofing therefore, not granting, that there was not fufficient evidence to convict the Begums either of rebellious actions or defigns, before an ordinary court of juftice in ordinary cafes, yet if the fituation of affairs was fuch, that either the public fafety muft be ruined, or fome facrifice or other made for its prefervation, it was the duty of Mr. Haftings to make fuch a facrifice: and if there was an option of facrifices, it was alfo his duty to fix on that which was the moft effectual for obtaining its end, and which could be made with the leaft violation, or appearance of violation, of juftice. But to refume the jaghires (an equi-

valent

valent being intended), and to feize the treafures of the Begums, was the moft effectual facrifice that could be made. It was alfo that which could be made with the leaft violation, or appearance of violation, of juftice; for there was at leaft a degree of probable evidence that thofe Begums entertained hoftile defigns againft the Englifh, and that they had even begun to carry them into execution : therefore, the meafures taken by Mr. Haftings on the emergency in queftion, were, in all refpects, the moft proper that could have been poffibly imagined. If they were improper, let the Englifh nation reftore their treafures to the Begums.

If in human nature there are qualities by which it is diftinguifhed from the animal creation, men are themfelves, in different climates, greatly diverfified : and they not only find in their condition the fources of variance and diffention, but they appear to have in their minds the very feeds of animofity, and to embrace the occafions of mutual oppofition with alacrity and pleafure; a conftitution of nature, which, in the myfterious courfe of Providence, gives room for the exercife of the nobleft virtues. From this diverfity among the different nations there arifes a diverfity in the modes by which they are governed. One form of government fuits
one

one country, and one another. The governments in Afia are defpotic, and it is by fum-
mary proceedings alone, and a ftrong arm, by
which, in their prefent moral condition, they
can be governed. To introduce new forms of
government into nations, if practicable at all, is
the work of time. Attempts were made to introduce liberty into Ruffia at once, but they proved abortive; and, in like manner, the fteps that
have been taken to introduce the Englifh law
into India have been attended with great con-
fufion, and been productive of much inconvenience
and mifchief. It is found difficult to govern the Hin-
doos by our laws even in times of profound peace.
What then was Mr. Haftings to do in times of in-
finite difficulty and danger ? In proportion to the
embarraffments of the Englifh, the ideas and pretenfions of the native princes of India naturally
revived. The novelty and the odioufnefs of our
inftitutions were more fenfibly felt ; the fanctions
by which they were eftablifhed were weakened ;
and all things feemed rapidly to revert to that
fituation in which we found India, when, under
the pretence of being the treafurers and tax-
gatherers of the Great Mogul, we extended our
power over fo many provinces of Afia. The
Britifh power in India was only of an artificial
kind,

kind, the whole mass of numbers and opinion of right being against it. If the truth must be told, it was purely despotic, and depended for its efficacy on the principle of FEAR. Should the pressure and weight of Government be lessened, the fire, which was smothered only by that weight and pressure, must break out with an explosion fatal to the oppressors. The feeble, the partial, and varying attempts that had been made to establish a new order of affairs, had not formed such a strength of Government as could be depended on in a new and unprecedented situation, big with danger and final destruction. The artificial mounds by which we had sometimes endeavoured, and might yet propose to confine and lead the stream of popular opinion, would give way to that storm which was ready to fall, and restore all things to their usual and their deepest channel. It is justly observed by the Roman historian Sallust, that dominion is easily preserved by the same means through which it was gained. On the occasion of an extrordinary and alarming conjuncture in India, the Governor-General of Bengal reverted to the principles by which our dominion there had been both acquired and supported, and provided for the public safety by expedients, which, in times of tranquillity, and in European Governments,

vernments, might be deemed violent and irregular, but which, in the circumſtances in which he
was placed, were proper, becauſe they were ſa-
lutary.

If ever a caſe exiſted in which a ruler of a people might aſſume a latitude of conduct ſuitable to
political exigences, Mr. Haſtings is juſtifiable in
the meaſures in queſtion, by all that can juſtify an
extraordinary ſtep in an extraordinary ſituation:
rectitude of intention ; the wiſe adaption of the
means to the end ; and complete ſucceſs. The
meaſures he purſued were not purſued for his own
emolument, (for Mr FRANCIS does not charge
him with a ſpirit of private avarice and rapine,)
but for the public ſafety. In reſuming the jaghires, and ſeizing the treaſures of the Begums,
he conſulted the public tranquillity, and by ſet-
tling on thoſe ſequeſtrated Princeſſes a yearly reve-
nue in money, inſtead of land, he provided for
their own. His adminiſtration has been crowned
with glorious ſucceſs: nor would a nation ſo generous as the Engliſh have been contented with
merely abſtaining from all criminations of ſo ami-
able a private, and ſo great a public character, if
private reſentment, indefatigable labour, and the
utmoſt acuteneſs of underſtanding, had not combined to exhibit a malignant and partial view of his
actions

actions in detail, inftead of tracing the mutual con-
nections and contemplating the refult of the whole.

For of what, my countrymen, is Mr. Haftings accufed? Not of fnatching the morfel
from him that is ready to faint: not of tear-
ing the fcanty veftment from fhivering limbs:
not of extorting by refined torments, like a Cortez
or Pizarro, or fome of our own nation, whofe
names the imagination of the reader will readily
fupply, hoarded treafures for fwelling a private fortune; but, at the very worft, for faving an empire
by irregular means. Who, henceforth, will nobly
dare to break through the reftraints that malice
and cabal, armed with the chicanery of law, im-
pofe on every mind that is more anxious about
felf-intereft than the public profperity and fafety?
Shall it henceforth be neceffary, for the conduct of
our diftant concerns, to fend out the Judges of
Weftminfter-hall, or his Majefty's Solicitor and
Attorney-General? What is to be our fituation
in Afia, if our affairs are directed in that quarter of
the world, not by the towering genius of Warren
Haftings, but the creeping caution of Pepper Ar-
den? In the fuccefsful, I will add, in the mild
meafures adopted by the Governor-General, was
there ought repugnant to the fpirit by which our
dominions in India had been uniformly governed?

The

The conditions on which our territorial property in India was transferred to the East-India Company, were indeed plausible, but those conditions were not observed. The king of Delhi granted certain rights to the Company, on condition of their paying that tribute which he was unable to raise from the refractory Nabobs of the Mogul empire. But if he was unable to enforce his demands on the native Princes of India, he was still less able to enforce them on the Company, armed with the troops and the navies of Britain. The Company exacted the tribute from the Princes, but with-held it from the Emperor. They violated their engagements, and pursued a system of rapine. Nor let it be said that these were the acts of the Company only: the British Government were accomplices in their schemes; they defended them by their power, and they shared in the plunder. The East-India fair trade was hardly able to support itself. It was the territorial property, and the private fortunes acquired in India, that made this trade beneficial to the nation at large, and which alone enabled the Company to pay the annual sum stipulated with Government. It cannot be concealed that this was the real ground on which our affairs stood in India, and this the principle on which they were conducted. The

Governor

Governor General reprefented the Genius of Bri-
tannia in the Eaft, which was not fmiling and
foft, but commanding and auftere. If to maintain this tone was a crime, it was not the crime
of him in whofe perfon it centred, and by whofe
fidelity to his engagements it was difplayed.
No, my countrymen, it was not Mr. Haftings
that was reduced to the neceffity of over-awing
by feafonable feverities the rebellious defigns of
the Rajah of Benares and the Begums of Oude,
and crufhing in the bud a general revolt in India.
It was our mifmanagement and difafters in the
Weft: it was our love of gain and ambition in
the Eaft: it was the combination of the world
againft us, that obliged the man in whofe hands
our fafety was entrufted, to ufe the beft means in
his power for its prefervation. It was faid of
old,

Quod fi violandum jus, regnandi caufa violandum eft.

This maxim was not delivered in defence of
cruel and wanton ambition. It imports, that, as
political government is the greateft bleffing of
human fociety, it is to be preferved and main-
tained at all adventures. Every political grie-
vance may be remedied by a nation while it pof-
feffes the force and fpring of legiflative authority:
but

but when that is loft, all is loft. Were the intentions of Great Britain, then, towards the natives
of India humane and gracious ?   The light and
temporary diftreffes of the Princeffes of Oude
was a cheap price for fo great a purchafe : for I
affume it as a maxim, that, without that facrifice,
the power of Britain in India muft have been an-
nihilated.   But this would not have happened
without a ftruggle : fo that the queftion that Mr.
Haftings had under confideration was, Whether,
when the fortune of Great Britain ftood trembling
on a precipice, and the ftrongeft probabilities (if
our lawyers impugn the denomination of *legal
evidence*) exifted, that the Begums of Oude had
taken the firft fteps of revolt, whether he fhould
follow the courfe he in fact purfued ; or, by yield-
ing to the inevitable neceffity of a mutiny, or of
difbanding the army, cut off the hopes of a political reform in India, by cutting off the power of
England on which it depended, involve the whole
country in anarchy and bloodfhed, expofe the
Englifh to the revenge of the natives, and render
the final diffolution of our power in the Eaft as
violent and painful, as its firft commencement
was plaufible, and its progrefs profperous ?   In
fuch a dilemma, could the rigour of juftice, could
the tendernefs of mercy, condemn even fuch an
expedient as that which was reforted to by the

Marquis.

Marquis of Fauquieres in the confederate war, in the reign of queen Ann ? The Marquis was sent out, at the head of a party which was to pass in the night through a wood in deep silence, and to perform a service which required equal secrecy and expedition, and on the performance of which the very salvation of the French army depended. Towards the morning, but while it was yet dark, one of the men under his command began to cough violently, and could not by his utmost efforts suppress that irresistible convulsion. The commander sacrificed the life of one man to that of thousands *. The French nation lamented the hard fate of the innocent man ; but did not condemn the action of the general. Compare with this deed the conduct of Mr. Haftings in Oude, and the innocence, and even services of the French soldier, with the hostile intentions and preparations of the Begums; and say, if either, which was the most to be condemned ?

In a critical and biographical introduction to an history of the reigns of King William and queen Ann, by Mr. Alexander Cunningham, the English Resident at Venice, just published, and which, I trust, will be read and studied by every man who is a friend to the liberty, who

* See Fauquieres' Memoirs.

de

delights in recollecting the pureft and moft glorious times of our republic, and is difpofed to
watch the many-formed ambition of France : in
the Introduction, I fay, to that hiftory, there is
an anecdote recorded of the great Prince Eugene, which I fubmit to the confideration of the
accufers of Mr. Haftings. At the battle of
Malplaquet, while victory yet hung in fufpence,
a youth of the name of James Campbell (afterwards General Sir James Campbell, of Laurs),
at the head of a party of horfe, fprung forward
out of the line, cut through the enemy, and even
the Gens d'Armes of France, and through again
to the confederate army. This daring action
ftruck a panic in the French, infpired our men
with courage, and decided the fate of the day.
Certain officers of our army murmured againft
Campbell, and were fevere in their cenfures of
his conduct. But Eugene, who, as the writer
of the Introduction obferves, conceived that a
conjuncture might exift wherein the tranfgreffion
of rules might imply the higheft degree of merit,
thanked him for having fo nobly and fuccefsfully
exceeded his orders, on the day after the battle,
at the head of the army. Is the power of France
lefs now than it was then ? Is her ambition, though
better concealed, lefs dangerous ? Is the merit

of

of Haftings lefs than that of Campbell ? No ! but an Eugene is wanting to proclaim his juft praife in the face of his enemies.

But it was not only India that Mr. Haftings faved to the Britifh empire. The conquefts that were made there, by the valour of the Britifh troops under his government, were exchanged, at the late peace, for other places, which, but for thofe conquefts, muft have remained in the hands of our enemies. Now, Mr. Fox, and others of his party, as Major Scott told them in their teeth without being contradicted, about two months before the peace was concluded, declared in the Houfe of Commons, that without a peace of fome kind or other this nation was undone. A peace as honourable and advantageous to Great Britain as her fituation could poffibly leave room to expect was concluded ; and immediately Mr. Fox and his friends, who had fo often devoted Lord North to the block, unite for the purpofe of turning the man out of his office, by whom the peace was made. So that both the man who made the peace, and the man who, by the vigour of his adminiftration in the Eaft, enabled him to make it, without facrificing our Weft India Iflands captured by the French, are rewarded, the one with the lofs of office, the other

other with an unprecedented and ridiculous, but vexatious perfecution!---Never furely were fervices fo ill requited as thofe of Mr. Haftings to this country. In private life he was the friend, and patron, and bountiful affiftant of thoufands, devolved by their friends on fortune and on his goodnefs. In his public character he faved India by the gentleft facrifice that was ever yet made by prince or ruler in circumftances fo full of alarm and danger: yet this is the man of whom Mr. Burke fays, that " it is indecent that " he fhould be permitted to go about at large, " enjoying the common benefits of liberty, frefh " air, and focial life."

As I introduced thefe obfervations on the charges brought againft Mr. Haftings by his enemies, and on the arguments by which they are fupported, with a great name, to whofe character and fortune thofe of that gentleman bear a ftriking refemblance; fo I fhall, in like manner, conclude them, by remarking a fimilarity between his conduct, on his return from India, and that of another great fpirit, when his fortune and fate were committed to the general opinion and determination of the Englifh nation. " While " the fucceffion was yet unfettled, King William " entered into no intrigues either with the
" electors

" electors or the members of parliament; and
" so far was he from forming cabals with the
" leaders of parties, that he disdained even to
" bestow caresses on those whose assistance might
" be useful to him*." Admirals have lost oppor-
tunities, Generals have lost armies, and Commanders in Chief auspicious conjunctures and
times never to be recalled; but they threw them-
selves into the scale of opposition, and were
loaded with offices and honours. Mr. Hastings,
the saviour of the nation, courts not the favour of
any party, but looks confidently to the nation for
justice. It might have become Administration,
as well-wishers to the support of the British Government, to have shewn so much countenance
at least to the cause of Mr. Hastings, as to have
used their influence, which prevails so much in
other matters, in order to obtain a patient hearing
to the evidence and arguments urged by Mr.
Burgess, Mr. Nicholls, Major Scott, and others.
The little jealousy and cunning of the Minister
of the day begin already to be generally sus-
pected, and the motives which directed his voice
against Mr. Hastings to be understood. I trust
to the generosity of the English nation, that

---

* Hume's History of England.

the

the meannefs of that iniquitous policy will one day be made manifeft; that it will lay the name with the power of that *cunning youth*, low in the duft, and ferve as a foil to difplay the magnanimous virtue of Mr. Haftings, concerning whofe praife no tongue or pen that defcribes the prefent, in any future times, fhall be filent. Were it not that the example of his ill-requited merit may ftrike its roots too deep into the hearts of other commanders, and that the enemies of our country will triumph over us, I fhould almoft rejoice that fo great, fo well regulated, and compofed a mind as that of Mr. Haftings, has found, like the glorious objects of *antient oftracifm*, in the perfecution of his countrymen, the nobleft theatre of virtue, and the loudeft trumpet of fame. And yet the vote of the Houfe of Commons on the 8th of February, and particularly that of one man, I cannot reflect on without furprize and indignation. I do not wonder that the warm imagination of Mr. Burke is over-heated by fo long and clofe an attention to one object. I do not wonder that Mr. Sheridan, though of a difpofition naturally honeft, generous, and noble, fhould, from political views, act the part fo wifely committed to his powers by his political friends: far lefs do I wonder that even

I   he,

he, who in such suspicious circumstances abandoned the inquiry into the affair of Rumbold, and who had acknowlegded so emphatically, that, but for the exertions of Mr. Haftings, India must have been loft, I do not wonder that he who had no character for confiftency to lofe, fhould fit filent amidft the criminations againft the man whom he had praifed, and fneak off under the fhadow of the minifterial wing to vote againft him: but I wonder, that Mr. Pitt, who owes his ftation to the friends and to the perfonal magnanimity of the Governor General, in refufing to purchafe his *quietus* by joining a faction againft him; I wonder that Mr. Pitt, who pretends to ftand folely on the confidence of his countrymen, fhould fo meanly and fo impolitically defert that great man to whofe influence and virtue he owes his power, and his country its fafety. Do you wifh, young ftatefman, by fuch truckling conduct, to gain the good opinion and friendfhip of your opponents? There is a generofity in the nature of Fox, of North, of Burke, and Sheridan, which will never coalefce with the cunning of yours. Though the fortune of political war has placed thefe men in the oppofite lines, their hearts and minds are congenial with thofe of Haftings. Are

you

you fo weak, notwithftanding all that is taught by the law of nature, and even by the facred Scriptures, as to plead fcruples of confcience? Go then, exchange fituations with Doctor Prettyman, abandon the government of a great nation, and preferve the peace of your mind by relinquifhing your power, not by facrificing your friend. But is there not fomewhat of jealoufy at the bottom of your oppofition to Mr. Haftings? The world thinks fo; and, I believe, your countrymen will foon convince you that they do.

The perfecutions carried on againft great and good men, and the triumphs of the wicked and weak, with which the Englifh hiftory, and efpecially in its lateft periods, abounds, fhew how unworthily popular favour may be gained, and how undefervedly loft; how quick thofe tranfitions from one extreme to another, which are incident to popular governments; and with what caution and referve we ought to yield our affent to the doctrines of the day, or our approbation to the meafures of the moment, the true motives of which are feldom avowed, although plaufible pretexts are eafily found for recommending them to the multitude, who, from malignity, from a love of innovation and amufement, and from the very fociability of their nature,

ture, are eager to catch and fwell whatever tone
happens to be uppermoft for the time, which
originates for the moft part in private and unjuftifiable views, and which is circulated at firft
by felfifh induftry, and at laft by the tides of
fympathy and currents of popular paffion. But
thefe tides and currents fooner or later fubfide,
and return by a natural and neceffary reflux in
an oppofite direction ; *fometimes,* as in the general forrow which followed the death of So-
crates, even to a point when unavailing repen-
tance manifefts itfelf in acts of outrage and mad-
nefs. It is not until fuch tumults are calmed
that the characters of men are juftly eftimated,
and their names duly embalmed in the faithful
page of hiftory.

F I N I S.